LITANY

LITANY

SCOTT SONDERS

CARAVAN PRESS, LOS ANGELES, 1987

ACKNOWLEDGMENTS: Some material contained herein has been revised from RAZOR CANDY by Scott Sonders, Caravan Press, 1983, and has been reprinted with permission. Other poems have previously appeared in *L.A. Weekly, San Francisco P.M., The Venice Beachhead, Ha'am, ORT, The Activist, The Montreal Gazette, The Jerusalem Post, Poetry Magazine, Carolina Quarterly, Shirim, The Messenger, L.A. Reader,* and *The Herald Tribune.*

LITANY was partially underwritten by THE 1985 EDGAR LEE MASTERS NATIONAL AWARD FOR POETRY.

Cover Photos (back) are of Scott Sonders.

I.S.B.N. 0-912159-11-1

Library of Congress Catalog Number: 86-73071

Caravan Press
343 S. Broadway
Los Angeles, California 90013
(SAN 264-7222)

FOR THOSE OPPRESSED
BY THINGS OF BEAUTY.

CONTENTS

FLESH POEMS

WARM KISSES FROM COLD PLACES

THE DOWNSIDE OF DAYDREAMS

GENESIS AND RESURRECTION

FLESH POEMS

"[Woman] is bone of [Man's] bone and flesh of his flesh:
That is why Man and Woman love,
to become again as one."

—Genesis 2:23-24

"There are places within a man
No woman can ever know
Where he can never take you
And you mustn't ask to go."

—Author Unknown

CORNERS

no corners
no corners
i want to live
where there are no corners
and streets never end

where no one gets crossed
and nothing gets lost
where words don't bend
with hidden innuendo

i want to live
round as the world
where lines never begin
or end

no corners
no corners
i want to live
where there are no corners.

SOLILOQUY

sometimes i wish
i were a bird,
with wings that could
take me anywhere,
for nothing.

FLASHBACK

we laughed
over grapefruit and vodka
and promises of great sex
and you asked
if i'd be your slave
but then, i am already

and so i'm giving up for you
my shakespeare sits on the page
and you lay in my head
where hamlet should be

and now i recall
your weight in my arms
so pick the spot
on the map of your body
that will tempt us
past reservation
and i will meet you there.

MIDNIGHT, ROME: 10/1/86

christiana
where are you now
and whose name are you using tonight

what gifts will entice you
and how many toys will it take
before another falls in love with you

christiana
teutonic goddess of cold, brazen beauty
and hidden warm heart where you hang
a stone and turn your head
with closed eyes while
you service without a smile

christiana
where were you then
when i was inside of you

i would pay one hundred times
your price to know

and what were you then
when i presented you with the carved
crystal butterfly that made you cry
though you tried not to

christiana
i would trade a week
of your services for one
long kiss from your secret mouth
that no one ever shares
the unexplored lips
that long to be touched
and the cheeks yet virgin

christiana
you are only nineteen
the sign of the crab
how deep will you swim
to lose yourself in the dark waters
safe beneath a surface of stolen, golden
hair that you sell nightly

how many times must you be violated
before you finally dream of me

christiana
whose name are you using tonight
while i sit alone
in this darkened room in rome
looking through a lighted window
where the pretty english girl
is drying her body
with a stiff, white towel

christiana
i will try again to sleep soon
with the stains of dead mosquitos
dancing on the peeling paint

i will try to dream something nice
for the english girl

and for you christiana

for if you were here with me now
this room would have no walls anymore.

HAIKU

temple then empty
yet for death
and that low sound
of one page turning.

LINES

before making
any final decisions
about me, ladylove

let us sit
in bright sunlight
so you can stare
at the lines
in my face.

BLOOD COOKIES
[Montreal: May 20, 1982]

...for Irving Layton: Tightrope Dancer

a wedding of explosion and flame
ripped across the fourteenth floor
and tossed a floral bouquet
of broken mirrors to the street below
and the onlookers covered their heads
with umbrellas and crossed arms
cradled by that night
of brittle stars and crystal glass

i dressed carefully
took passport, wallet and lover
then started down the stairs, thinking
of musicians playing for time in dachau
and of poets wordless from smoke
that churned in perfect german ovens
and of dancers with torn feet
and of anne frank, joan of arc
brothers and sisters corroding
into bellowing clouds of soot

and i thought of you
old / poet / jew
sitting on a greek beach
still burning with music and holocaust
farting retsina and feta cheese
and getting laid after seventy years
because you are
an old / poet / jew

so when that funeral pyre conceded
i gathered my thirtyish
poet / jew / self
with my twentyish french lover
back to my room yet scorched and piquant
where we lay locked in a fiery dance
until dawn also ignited
and left us consumed
two old / poet / jews.

PRAYER ON THE BORDER

i am learning
to be fragile again
receptive
and embarrassed

i am a glass moth
flying
out of reach.

WE SHOULD ALL BE HEROES TO SOMEONE

"Now Joseph was handsome and well favored, And his master's wife saw this and said: Make love to me."

—Genesis 39:6-7

captured by gypsies
i lived in many places
before the age of five

i could perform wonders
with sleight of hand
and was skilled at magic
while yet eleven

i was a political prisoner
and savvy in song
when a girl committed suicide
to celebrate seventeen

i was a cabalist
a perfect master
and a metaphysical wizard
before i drew twenty-two

then i broke the chain
of sinless crime, escaped
the slavery of space and time
and knew god by twenty-nine

i am thirty-three now and dangerous
jesus became christ at thirty-three
follow me, and you
will become a burning apostle

if you were meant to be gypsy or lord
you would have known long ago.

GHETTO BLASTERS

the crowd was satisfied and went home
barney was stretched out
on the park bench, head laid back
like he was resting from a game of dominoes

but i could see he was dead
grey faced and stiff
life leaving his body
like sand in a three minute egg timer
a cavernous hole in the chest
where his heart used to be, gaping
like the red slit between darla's steamy thighs
always ready, always hot and big
enough to crawl into and get warm
enough to escape the freezing pain

i wanted to stick my numb hands
in the gaping red slit of barney's chest
and feel around for his eye color
before the brain was paralyzed
to try and follow a slippery artery
leading like a line on a roadmap to where
i could stop feeling cold and numb and lost

i had told him, lighten up man,
the welfare check'll come today
but he did not lighten up
went out instead and got dusted
like a crazy motherfucker of a junkyard dog
with his muzzle lathered for a close shave

and then the law came with sirens screaming
and cherry lights spinning like wine sick ballerinas
and a gale of blue serge swept over barney
like white on rice, ripping
his naked black body into the air
where it hung for a heartbeat
then sank like a popped balloon
as a .38 hollowpoint pulverized
his big warm heart into
a couple pounds of cold dead meat

they said he was dangerous
baby jesus, how could
that bad, crazy bro be dangerous

i heard it said that barney
had jammed with jimi and coltrane
they were three slick dudes
really had some moves

but now i hear them on the ghetto blasters
and hope those boys aren't stuck
in some jive, rock 'n' roll heaven
that might as well be hell

so play those ghetto blasters loud, man
don't let it get too heavy, turn it up

barney, your war is over
you can strut your stuff for angel chicks now
so turn it up, turn it up
turn it all the way up
cause i can still hear the screams.

DISEASE

and there was a woman with leather skin
who spoke eloquently
yet bled her love on fields of paper snow
like loud splashes of orange chalk

vulnerable only with a typewriter
sharing her disease with any man
she could suck like a thick, wood pencil
mutations for her yet unpublished novel.

BIRTH CERTIFICATE

do not probe my astrology
i have none

i was torn
from the pocket of a cripple

assembled
by blind women from scraps

built of blood
from the lips of a priest

i am not the issue of any womb
no pound of flesh was paid

so do not ask for names
from this orphan

they are
unspeakable.

THE SKIN HAS A MEMORY

last night was a washout
two clowns skipping like stones
over pools of dry chablis
ripples that never intersected
cerebral until it hurt
and the pain sat us straight
stiff and formal
cardboard cut-outs
hyphenated by candlelight

you should put more cunt in your poetry
then your fat thighs would melt
and sizzle like bacon
and you'd know about open heart surgery
and the taste of blood in your mouth

you should put more cunt in your poetry
and fill the words with come
make your nipples warm
and touchable like ripe raspberries

go to a city where none know your name
let your cunt do all the thinking
and fill your skin with memories

lock yourself in a hotel room
with a dozen dirty magazines
and every poem erica jong ever wrote

put your fingers deep within you
over and over
then rub them on your typewritter
and massage the stiff white paper

and when at last
your eyes are glazed & wild
and your words are lean & hungry

return to me
and speak the memories of your skin.

NOT LOST IN NEON STARS

she plays my ribs
like a golden xylophone
with lips that number every breath
this idol with eyes of tourmaline
who lies pinned to my linen sheet
a butterfly deified in glass

and the pearl moon stalks
a crooked tree now empty of cats
then leaps through our window and tears
the screen like a bloodless virgin

so cold and contemptuous
these showgirls undressed of white feathers
dancing across curtains of indigo lamé
and yet not lost in neon stars.

THE MANNEQUIN AND THE KITE

i build kites that sing
that sing, that sing
i build kites that sing for the wind

i build kites that sing
and are bullet-proof
that a mannequin cannot buy
with her smile of wood or coins of grace
placed on a cadaver's eye

i build kites that tease
narrow fingers of god
slice thin scars in sky
come from never but go forever
these kites they sing on high

i build kites that sing for the wind
i build kites that fly for free
and these kites they sing
they sing, they sing
these kites will sing for thee.

ILLUMINATIONS OF
ONE MAN'S HEART

i am undressed
but for your touch
unseen
without your eyes

i have no fruit
but for your mouth
no child
without your thighs

i am not light
but for your dark
not sun
without your shadow

i am not life
but for your death
i am no hero
without you.

THE PATRIOT

underwire bras
those implements of torture
are remnants of the inquisition
better to set the breast free
and hang like a proud silk flag
on a windless day

i'm a patriot you know
i salute flags and stand erect
for the national anthem

underwires though
remind me of quasimodo
they make me limp with dread
it's my gypsy blood
a genetic aversion to restraint
i get worried around chain link fences
and even the zoo makes me skittish

so keep your breasts free
i'm a patriot you know
i like proud silk flags.

HEAVEN'S GATE

i was a slave
chained to beauty
poured like molten gold
on heaven's gate.

A HEAT OF ANGELS

she disdained
the comfort of cocoons
and dreamed the dream
of butterflies that burst the sky
like a heat of angels

and with her eyes lost in laquer
she walked undressed
with bare feet on cold tile
wearing only a sense of urgency
and loss.

HAIKU

silence
is new snow
when cold crickets
stop chirping
and the starved leaves
fall.

THE BALCONIES OF PARADISE

somewhere in the south of france
and buried in a forgotten dream
the beach was green and fat
like a coiled snake, luminous
with rolls of oiled people

and the smell of jasmine was everywhere
as another heroin floated on the horizon
and perfume and sunlight washed the sand

and on the balcony of paradise
bubbles rose again in the syringe
like an animal breathing under sand
and the glass caught a gleam
from the liquid fire of autumn
and the steel spike in simone's arm
turned gold

and everything became warm and possible
and the window to god was hand cut crystal
and the crusty sheets
were satin.

WARM KISSES FROM COLD PLACES

"The heart has its reasons that reason knows nothing of."
—Blaise Pascal

"There is no habit quite so expensive as some women."
—Joan Rosenfeld

A LAST LETTER TO JIMI

There was a video remake of you on cable tonight. Only three minutes or so, but there it was: The Music. The *Machine Gun.* Burning skin off drums and tearing the breath from my chest. It felt like '66 again, when I worked the strobes at Kaleidoscope on Sunset. Ten feet from your axe. Dazed. Machine gun ripping splinters from wood stage floor. Smoking until I was transfigured. And later, you telling me you wanted to be with Jesus...but that was still a secret. Well, that was long ago and I stopped counting after John Lennon was buried. But now it's 4:00 AM and I've finished half a bottle of Martel cognac so I could say good night to you in style. So I could get stone free. So I could stop hearing the words to "Hey Joe": *Where you goin' to go? Where you goin' to run to now?* You were really asking yourself that question. You were asking us all. You were asking Jesus. You were asking me. And yes, I'm ripping you off shamelessly in this letter. But I have to. You said it all so well. And I can't even sing. And I hope you're okay now. That you found *some kinda way outa here.* Someway kinda good. Somewhere we all are not born jokers. Somewhere we all don't die thieves. You were a gentle soul. Too gentle. That's why you had to leave us. To become some kind of modern saint. Yeah, St. Jimi Of The Holy Order of Kick-Ass Guitar Men. So listen up all you imitation Princes. Lightweights. Nickel bag punks. Look out because St. Jimi is *comin' to get you now.* And as he sang so beautifully what Bobby Dylan wrote, *So let us not talk falsely now. / The hour is getting late.*

PHOTOGRAPHS

slices
of gem red blood

etched
in white satin paper

yielding
portraits

shaped
by shadow and light.

HELSINKI: 8/22/85

autumn comes ever quick now
wind grows strong
grows durable

chops of wave white slice
through fingertips of sea

sky oscillates masses of thunder
shot through then with iridescent
spasms of charcoal nimbus

tree leaves flutter like a thousand
dark green hummingbirds

and the air is a crisp linen sheet
sliding over the skin
like a shroud of winter

sasha is sometimes a shroud of winter
now trading a lump of ice
for the burning place
where once was heart

and her body shakes
while this stuff of blood
goes slow and cold and gray

much as these so close clouds
of helsinki twilight.

BAT WINGS AND
OTHER OFFERINGS

"Late, late yestreen I saw the new moon / With the old
Moon in her arms / And I fear, I fear, my Master dear /
We shall have a deadly storm."

—Ballad of Sir Patrick Spence

we are such grand old vampires
flying for blood and ruin
sucking the necks of hurricanes
drinking from ruby spoons

we taste exquisite grief
and suffer mortal loss
then abandon modern remedies
for a bloodless albatross

we fly from every deadly storm
watch old moons slip away
flap our wings like boney thunder
and keep the wolves at bay

with heart of emily dickinson
and hand of sylvia plath
we'll deal the cards and hope to win
this game of endless wrath

our master has a dozen names
at least as many games
to steal us back into his spell
and rage from where we came

the devil has his many shames
at least as many flames
to force us back to ice-cold hell
the grave from where we came.

GAUNTLETS OF THREADBARE SILK

i begin again
when mind and soul are through
to start the walk long down the hall
to lie alone and think of you

i begin again
when mind and soul are through
as my love for you
becomes more clean
less expressable
and my hands change
to gauntlets of threadbare silk
for your soft, hidden skin
that caused my soul to sing

i begin again
when mind and soul are through
trying not to break
what's been joined at the heart
and so i'm walking into you
with my eyes closed tight
and my chest open wide.

SILHOUETTE

that silhouette
beckoned yet
these harlequins
to hell
then called our name
and stole our clothes
and grinning
wished us well

now quiet
and so invisible
our covers were taken
so we, when maybe older
and mostly colder
would be a naked
and shameless three.

A LETTER TO M.

come back now
when all is end
to end
and tell me
what my name
was before

come back now
that these hands
are creased with longing
and my words
are only splashes of blood
over fields of white
linen paper.

LETTER TO M. #2

it was not knowledge or wisdom
that sent me breaking
empty bottles

it was not a day of clocks
dissolving
into a blur

it was not the ones who called me
cold or cool
at the wedding of our mutual friend

it was not your dark eyes
dancing like a storm tossed sea
that held the key to the mystery of dreams

it was not the sloping silk
of your shoulders suddenly bare
that made my mouth cotton dry and stammering

and i swear it was not even the tightness
in my stomach that told me
the heart's dead are never buried.

A RANSOM NOTE TO M.

in this room, now
empty of your voice

where once i wrapped
your naked arms with night

i learned no heart
is whole until it's broken

as your promise became
a puddle in the noonday sun

and every little death
got lost in rush hour

so yet i must hold
your letters for ransom

until this heart is paid
with hidden skin.

A SHORT REPLY

thank you
for adding
so much
to my life

you have made
forever
necessary

beyond love
longer than
everlasting

i need you
more than poets
can comprehend.

THE CAVE DWELLING OF GOD

i drift, the fat otter in cool blue
currents of mediterranean sea

and float on winding waterways
a lost bee with secret dreams

and watch the glow of moonfire
burn craters black in forest sky

yet so i return to the stillness
of subterranean shelter

this cave dwelling of god
sanctuary.

DESERT WHISPERS

pyramids crumble into carpets
of howling banshee sand
as the dromedary dawn
coughs a prayer to mecca

the magic of simple things
is not just simple magic

all that's alive
all that's dead
porcelain rock
and clouds of thread

i am this desert avatar
i am this song of the nile.

A VISION OF THE SEVENTH SON

"And Joseph said to the children of Israel, And God
will surely bring you out of this land. And he died
and was embalmed in a coffin in Egypt."

—Genesis 50:24-6

i dreamed while floating down the nile
of crowns and snakes and sceptres
i burned by day and prayed by night
with fever, priests and spectres

i wore a coat of dazzling color
on the cut of my devotion
four hundred years of history
drifted by in mystic motion

the sphinx conceded secret charms
of magic to mix with marrow
i brewed and gulped, it gave my legs
the strength to outrun pharoah

a sparrow flew in my bluest eye
a vision in my boneless face
a frog croaked in the wheatless fields
so the exodus took place

and i was joseph in a moonless tomb
with god and blood and potions
and dreams were sealed in the sacred ark
then carried to the land of goshen

i awoke a smoky avatar
the spirit in the mirror was he
that ghostly tomb was etched in glass
and his seraph was impaled in me.

HAIKU

that one heart now two
as others lay between them
and grief waits doglike.

LEGACY

for Sylvia Fradkin: August 1, 1982

in the past weeks
your already dead spirit
begged the cancer
to claim you completely

and it did

that radiant face
so full, fine and gentle
now yellow and sere
the smile lost in a chemical hell
and buried in furrows of pain

that lumbering debt of life
for fifteen years
i thought it would never end

the great weight you carried
never marred a secret pleasure
and your treasured dinners
brought us thanksgiving
and a garner of grace

now you lie somewhere strange and new
cancer stole your hair
and you stare with vacant eyes
at the long blue arms of god

i know you are cradled there
your weight and hurting are over
but i cannot help
still
wanting to hear
your song.

THE CHANGING

I

Winter had come white and hard to St. Jerome but Adrienne was stubborn. Her terrace had remained a defiant tango of tropical vines. And she stood there before the mirror, naked and grieving for her wasted flesh. She had not showered and the film between her clothes and skin had become a rare oil. The morning had again been long and slow with pain. The air around her was heavy and asphyxiating and her lungs sang in low, menacing tones. She coughed, wiped her mouth with the back of her forearm, ignored the streak of dark blood and looked over at the shoebox where she had placed the cockatiel. Its death made Adrienne shiver as she lifted the bird from its paper coffin and placed it on a silver hand mirror. The glass was cold as betrayal but the body was soft as moss and more shades of color than seasons can change. Its eyes were shut tight as a child's fist on candy, yet she continued to stroke its throat and breast, rocking back and forth well into midday. But then the ants came and she went out to the frozen earth and buried it. She never told me where.

That day was tattoo. I had seen her eyes shine even as her hands were raw and blistered from digging bare in the icy ground. I felt the power and glory she had stolen from her obsession. She was dying but would not resign. Her anger choked up in her throat and she yelled at the walls and cursed the heaviness of the air and the bloodiness of her spittle. The winter and the mirror and the bird had been omens. She threw her arms about her head, naked and dancing like a wooden marionette, the blood of her mother singing lethal in her old veins. Soon before dark, she quieted and I left.

You were ten years old then, your little enameled fists shaking like white pots of boiling eggs and your auntie Randye trying to explain that *grandmaman* would not be coming home again. And it was so that we watched Adrienne die. Her stoic pride now pleading for the morphine that could not begin to mask the hideous pain that chewed through her lips, mouth and upper half of her digestive tract. I had seen suicides before, none of them clean or pretty... but drinking Drano! I guess it was her epilogue: A statement about the extreme of things that were, and always would be.

44

II

In the fourth summer after that day of tattoo, your mother, who barely survived her own mother's death, sent you to stay with me for holiday. You spoke only French and I did not, yet still we laughed and talked. The perfect honeymoon, you pulling me back to frivolous times and me pushing you to adulthood. We never mentioned the suicide but there remained that tattoo of a shadow around your smile, even when I forgot our dinner and barbecued the chicken blacker than the cooking coals.

And another eight years went by and I was in Montreal again, standing in the alcove of your aunt's house, watching a baby tigershark provoke a slow swimming turtle. Randye and I were talking of things passed, of how we lay in bed on the night of the suicide and her body then was still young and hard and ignorant of death. And as we spoke of those things, you walked up the front steps, quiet as a sleeping angel and heard of that you already knew, but this freshness of old emotion made you feel like you were standing at the edge of a cliff. And you were fully afraid and that fullness made life more real and clear. And you laughed. And the family blood had ripened also in you. And you were your mother and your aunt. And you were your grandmother. And your ancestral beast sang to the violin of night.

And so Gina we became as lovers spending two capricious weeks eating ripened brie on long twists of sourdough. Drinking dusty bottles of dry, red wine beneath the statue of Frère Joseph. Believing that we alone knew love as no others could. And we slow waltzed to rock 'n' roll music in the discos on Clark Street.

But lovers and love don't always find each other. And three years later, your rare and recent letter tells me how you often lie alone and wait for love, and how you knew I was one you would lose. And you, *mon petite?* Have you carved complicated idols from simple stone? Religion is easy when all else fails. So do not be quick with worship. I am just flesh.

HAIKU

your touch unclothes me
and i am invisible
but then for your eyes.

TRANSFIGURATION

a copper apple
dangles from an ebony tree
where a windchime stutters
and a thin dog with one blue eye
growls in sympathy for the dead
or soon-to-be dead
and a heart of amethyst
swings in that leafless tree
where a blonde girl sits
playing for the moon
while bubbles of starlight
fall around her hair like sequins
and silver glitter
and she sings of metamorphosis
and slowly, slowly
i feel us changing
into implements of purest gold.

THE DOWNSIDE OF DAYDREAMS

*"In her first passion woman loves her lover,
in all others, all she loves is love."*

—Lord Byron

"The tragedy of love is indifference."

—W. Somerset Maugham

AT THE HONOLULU SKYLINE

this
   skyline
      of honolulu
         is a crowd
            of skyscrapers
               towers
                  dwarfed
               by mt. tantalus
            random nests
         in the muscles
      of the punchbowl
   and like those
sunken warships
drowning
   in the
      cerulean tide
         where coral beds
            rise from the powder
               and as so many fish
            without gills
         they wrench
      from that sea
         onto the sand
            and try
               to fly
                  skyward
            from
         the pearl
      harbor.

REQUIEM

this black soil now so alive
with a litany of eager worms
waiting for their meager feast
of cheeks that once blushed red
and the mourning morning
hallows fresh turned earth
with tears carved in sorry stone
as wooden walls enclose
the decomposing eyes of time
and a cadence rolls through sunlit fog
from a single staccato drum
and the loan taken from the side of man
is paid in full.

SEEDLESS GRAPES

the morning of her third birthday
we sat at the top of the stairs
and ate green grapes
cold and smooth
with no seeds
to catch in the space between teeth
i'd eat slowly
one, two, three
and give tiree the fourth
as she attempted nonchalance

her name was an echo of scotland
where her parents worked
mostly at the killing of rats
while the bagpipes moaned
for the rabid death
sequestered in low stone cairns
terriers are like that
careful for grapes and rats
and careless with birthdays

now only those stairs remain
blanched and bent
against a horizon of tall cedars
undaunted by the june heat
that rubs an eye
raw and almost crying
over terriers, grapes
and birthdays.

THE ESCAPE ROUTE

like a moth dancing
to the flaming pyre
and burning away its past
this is the heart of fire
addiction and the final slavery
escape is only in chains

and like a silk petal
praying in the satin rain
this is the eye of the hurricane
where flowers turn to gold
but escape is only in rust

and so as the jackal
running for the glacier moon
this is the star of june
the blinding light of god
escape is nowhere in sight

and like some cotton candy
melting in oceans of lollipop glee
this is the drowning guts of the sea
a mystery too deep to fathom
escape is but a watery grave

so now weave your mothy cocoon
and keep your flowers in seed
bark ever slowly at the moon
but you cannot escape or be freed.

ANTIBES ON SUNDAY MORNING

startled by a morning of february warmth
i soak in splendid sunlight
and trace places where lizard feet
are discreetly glued in concrete shoes

a rustle of rosemary leaves spicy gusto
on fingers of wind, and loud buzzing bees
[those cheap jasmine drunks]
kiss every wanton pistil
of blushing bougainvillea

and a shadow of lost plane
regains its footing on a cloud
squints with sunny surprise
then hums homeward with the bees

but the lizards stay with me, still
the russet male dipping into a push-up
and slowly blowing an iridescent bubble
to impress his chestnut ladylove
where we lay and pray in silent reverie
thawed and thankful
for every separate peace.

ON THE CALLING OF GOD
BY HIS NAME

god is dead
god is dead
i heard each argument
but nothing was said

and when at last
they cast the game
their name in stone
alone, remained

and so i know
as i survive
god is alive
god is alive.

MISSISSIPPI

relentless queen to a country
mainstream of dreams
topsoil poem to the midwest

flooding field with water
and heartland with blood
this liquid history of a nation

twisting still in st. louis
then winding down in new orleans
drunk on creme de menthe

where coffee-eyed creoles dance, dance
to the music of silver saxaphones
as the yellow mud river oozes
into the satin smooth crotch of liberty.

FORGIVE ME MY INHERITANCE

"Prepare war...for I will judge all the nations...
for the violence done to the Children of Judah."

—Joel 4:9-19

forgive me my inheritance
but god never died
sure some of us winced
some even cried
there were those who laughed
and those who lied
but god never died
there were tsadek high on cabala
who winked and laughed and knew
god never died
so forgive me my inheritance, vulture
go, flap your wings at another
deathcamp orgy
this blood is spoken for
reclaimed from egyptian mortar
if you please, so
forgive me my inheritance
but god never died.

SERENGETI

sparks of glory
from iron locomotives cascade
into black holes like exploded stars
and bantu natives
very brown and baptized
chant tanganyika, tanganyika

and the steel rails sing of love and rescue
and the dangerous things hot bellies do
when twisted by separation, or cold
and mombassa man with mojo stick
hunts nakuru juju, wet and black
and quivering as water waiting
under a new moon

and magic hieroglyphs
are carved into the luminous sand
in this land of redemption
by telephone wires that hang
like spider webs on wooden crucifixes

this, the land of cush where sheba held
a hebrew king in her ebony thighs
and the words, turn   turn   turn
were as sparks of glory
where in the ritual fire
there is no substitute for victory.

THE KILLING

go cut the stain of love
and be your own betrayer
as a haunted face remembers lace
with waves of wanton hair

now there's venom wine to drink
and flesh to slice between
a cruel orgy of coathangers
where once there was a dream

and scars are turning hearts to smoke
where souls were singed but free
and the blaze of love is a tree on fire
and desire's the flame of need

so when this bitter truth is told
a different child might learn
to never put its faith in love
or anything that burns.

A CANDLE FOR MORPHEUS

in this oh so quiet, oh so quiet
wooden flesh of night
my eyes are like an owl
rivets of light, drilling quiet holes
in the wooden flesh of night
narcotic of mercy
sleep doesn't come
eyelids are lost moths
fluttering in light
to tranquilize pain, and satisfy
cannibals gnawing at my brain
in the wooden flesh of night

hunchbacked, camouflaged
twisted and insane, i learn to sing
i learn to write, i learn to laugh
at wax black night, this wax black
candle burning to its middle
in a wisp of smoke and light, where
a lisping word is born and another
stuttering line is added to my face
in the wooden flesh of night

and in this oh so quiet, oh so quiet
shadow of light, i will die awake
another story shaking in my fist
and my lips curled in spite
so let my children be carpenters
carving out their sleep
from the wooden flesh of night.

SITTING DUCKS

with lips furled like sails
and curled over the edge
of an iced glass of pernod
and creme de menthe,
she hissed between
a thin smile and spit out
her astrological sign:
cunt with bitch rising,
she said, and my moon
never shines for free

and so it is understood
tongues that suck cool
goblets of chinese jade
have been trained as whores
to emperors,
and storytellers
rich only in metaphor
pay for a quick embrace
by changing into clay pigeons
that are shotgunned
like sitting ducks.

MELTED DIAMONDS

the frenzy of crickets
exploded
in the hot night
undiluted by darkness
and the sky
was transparent obsidian
swirling with stars
that seemed
as melted diamonds

and those diamonds
stay transfused
in my veins
with every memory
of the skin round
her breasts pressed
so hard to my ribs
that i saw
how first adam felt
when god cleaved
eve from his side
and their bodies then
forever hungered
to rejoin.

LITANY

in the slow, slow
shadows of the moon
we danced within
a show of starlight
and slowly so it came
we did not know
we did not know.

I HAVE MADE YOU IMMORTAL

many
give passion
and body

some
pay money
and mind

few
will give
love

but
with only these
words

one
had made you
immortal.

THE EDGE OF THE WORLD

I. Prelude

i have come to the edge of the world
lightheaded as a cork bobbing in wine
soon to be eighteen
nearly one third dead
and the pain has already started
as i hear elvis singing
and april's voice is low and cold
recalling t.s. eliot's warning
that april is the cruelest month
yesterday was april
today is april
i pray for may
for may has pelicans in new red shoes
skipping like young sailors in the fog
sloshing as they walk on the waves

II. Baptism

and onward
those pelicans and me
perched on the edge of the world
that window ledge of eighteen
leading to a sea of rolling coils
slithering to the shore
like a green-eyed serpent
thrashing off withered skin
like useless kelp on the beach
old sandcastles for young flies

and the electric rain was hissing
hissing, kissing
the snaking power lines
on a thick jetty of granite
that thrust into the ocean
erect, wet and steady
splashing alabaster foam
into the womb of the sucking sea

and those pelicans and me
we sat, lonely fishermen in the waves
apostles receiving baptism
rattling our bones at may
and dancing on the skeleton wind

and so the hissing faded
and the wind and the sea
and the pelicans and me
stared at the muscular hills
and knew that we were holy
quietly holy, rock footed
red shoed, wetly sexed
wholly holy, so very wholly holy

and so we huffed and puffed
and moved from the distant thunder
onward and holy
with the hollow madness of eighteen

III. Confirmation

and i left them there
by the rocks and the sea
because i was almost old
and needed the cure
that she hid between her thighs

and onward
i left the old revolution
for the new revelation
and the city
of paper-doll-cut-out fantasies
and my stilted verses that simply didn't sing
and the paths of glory
where the only heroes were dead heroes
where scarecrows died on walls of graffiti
and marble statues were for pigeon stools
and no matter what i did
the heroes just stayed dead

and onward
i went with christian brothers
tin soldiers and wood sisters
who danced with skinny whores
who fought for tired patrons
and modeled for fat matrons
while pinocchio tried to be a real boy
but never ever knew
the aroma of a real woman

and onward
with plaster-of-paris-figurines-
that-glowed-in-the-dark-
and-said-i-loved-you-
sealed-with-a-kiss

and onward
and onward
and the heroes just stayed dead

IV. Anthem

so i followed the hollow madness of eighteen
walked to the rim of june
and plunged into summer, tumbled
and clawed the sides of the month
trying to put the brakes on
trying to stop the fall
trying to slow the rush of days
but i fell only deeper
slipping on the smooth weeks of june
hitting bottom in july
and july almost killed me

and so i was, eighteen
and dazed and a red-eyed angel
sang to me through perfumed smoke
and showers of flower wine

and when i quivered off to sleep
in the sweet smell of her body heat
i dreamed of a house with thirteen rooms
with seven witches and six brooms
who circled there a large black pot
and boiled bits of spider's heart
then far away on the cold wet ground
i felt this odd pulsing sound
of knobby hands slowly clapping
whap, whap, whap
and cloven feet quickly tapping
rap, rap, rap
and then i spied a footless soldier
with april hanging from his shoulder
and the witches fled, gone for broke
like august leaves in flame and smoke

then i woke in september
and tried to remember the dream
of how it felt to become eighteen
yet sitting there upon my bed
with arms crossed over her head
was one remaining witch, naked
and hitched to the red-eyed angel
and in raspy gaspy harmony they sang
do not be tricked by jennifer snick
or carry your cross up stairs
wear an albatross about your neck
or a laurel leaf in your hair
don't bleed aloud or suffer in sin
thick souls may save your feet
from dead end paths or broken glass
lost women or one way streets
there are always witches and angels
who will ache and ask your trust
yet are craven in their emptiness
so be careful with your lust
now smell our damp arousal
hear these prayers we leave for free
remember ever our sizzling touch
but keep your voice in a heavenly key

then poof, poof
the witch and the angel, whichever was which
vanished in the twitch of any eye
so onward with their song
and onward with their trick
and on with learning and burning
and building with blood and brick

then there came a cackle, cackle
where hensfeet crackled in the dust
hnnff, hnnff they scratched at worms
hnnff, hnnff they caught them firm
then there came a pig, pig, pig
oh feel it squeel, souiee
and the clock did a ticka, tick, tick
while a saint smoked dope for free

and a brooding dream arose
tissue paper light in the night
and the week-end face in sunday shoes
sweated vinegar, and thought yet
of brittle monday blues
and rusted muscles beyond repair
moaned with bones in worried defeat
yet october did rise and melt despair
with leafless lips upon my cheek

V. Carthage Revisited

and onward
i chanted each prayer three times eighteen
[hah, a clever stone image of diety]
refrained my voice to a heavenly key
changed places with those pelicans
wore new red shoes and rearranged my face
so as not to be recognized

and i moved onward, somewhere new
somewhere between this and that
where twenty tangled bodies sat
protesting, and playing for time

and they
merrily, merrily squeeled and clucked
merrily, merrily dodged and ducked — [sing]
merrily, merrily passed the buck
so early in the morning

and onward
where flies drank sour mash
from the lips of dying bums
on the sidestreets near interstate one
where empty bottles burned tattoos
on broken hearts and busted hands
where a little smoke and a little joke
and a poke in the arm with hepatitis
would add a little death
to an otherwise dull existence

and onward
where porno queens boogalood down broadway
and pimps sailed the flat black ocean
with hot crotched ladies, who pleased
or teased with kinky delicacy

and i watched and was confused
and turned to piss on a waiting bush
and i heard the seasons change as i pissed
and heard a young girl in the back of a '63 chevy
taste her first hot squirt of paradise
forgetting ms. gloria steinham
and the revolution, and the boogaloo
now she, was the porno queen
and what made the lava gush

and i heard the chevy radio sing gospel
oh testify

he is the wind that makes you happy
oh clap your hands
he is the wind that frees our people
oh hallelujah
he is love for evermore

then i recalled the seven witches
and tried not to sing out of key
and moved onward from the distant thunder
where heaven could remember my name

VI. Moses Comes To The Mountain

i have come to the edge of the world
and learned of freedom
too big a word for many to remember
and learned of love
four letters, almost cliche
and learned of how, where, when
and why, they never change
merely rearrange

and i learned of what
which is deeper wounds and wider scars
what, is getting older and laughing now
at the things that used to break your heart

no one ever figured out
how, and even trying for
why can make you crazy
where and when are matters of mere statistic
only what really counts
what, is right now

and now the years will be easier
i'll glide through every april
return to the sea of red-shoed pelicans
and know where to move when i hear the thunder

do you hear me now
i have come to the edge of the world
i have learned to sing in a whisper
almost old
almost nineteen
onward, onward, onward — [sing soft & slow]
do you hear me now
i have come
to the edge
of the world.

NOTES FROM HELL

First winter light crawls through the window like a nervous cat. My body is filled with pain and cheap wine, and the room with a vague, splashing sound. It is a seashell held to my ear by the neon pallbearer on a Virginia Slims billboard. It is the electric hum of platinum cotton over honed jade: The death chant of mosquitoes with eyes iridescent and bulging as they plead for redemption.

And my spleen is mean spirited from the evening before, wasted on yellowing photos exhumed from a shoebox grave. Old Polaroids of Nancy Zolchik when we shared Grade Three. And she was gypsy-eyed and wild. And we'd go behind the clapboard bungalows where she'd drop her white, cotton panties. And she'd allow my fingers in her naked pinkness. And it was wet and fragrant as Bordeaux. And I wonder where she is now, that sister of mercy with eyelids from a stone goddess and belly of Chinese silk. Did she ever give up to the heart of the night or get addicted at 4 AM? Rimbaud did. So did Hemingway when he blew his brains out with a 12-gauge shotgun. Addiction is like fingernails on a chalkboard. A noise you want to forget, like the pounding of your chest after intercourse or the twinge that whispers in your left arm before a heart attack: The echoes of death in your ear. Oh the shaking will stop with morphine or alcohol or barbiturates. But it is the precipitate of fear, so pristine, that makes us dance the razor's edge. And there we discover what makes our lives worthwhile. But then the stitches in my face are too close and sleep is too far, and a 10 mil. valium would feel like the Holy Grail. So I'll empty another glass of wine and try to forget Simone and her calling from Paris to say her French pussy was still inflamed with American poetry. My guess would be closer to generic yeast.

And the room now is luminous with light and the pain in my head has not subsided. Today I will finish this letter but the rent will stay unpaid. It will not be a good morning.

GENESIS & RESURRECTION

"It is better to die on your feet than to live on your knees."

—Emiliano Zapata

"Revolution begins with the misfits."

—H.G. Wells

"To die...so young to die...no, no, not I / I love the warm and sunny skies / Light songs & shining eyes / I want no war no battle cry / No, no...Not I. // But if it must be that I live today / With blood and death on every hand / Praised be He for the grace, I'll say / To live, if I die this day / Upon your soil, my home, my land.

—Hannah Senesh
Nahalal, 1941

Hannah Senesh [1921-44], poet and Haganah fighter who, after parachuting into Nazi-occupied Europe to rescue Allied prisoners and organize Jewish resistance, was captured, tortured, and executed by a German firing squad.

DEDICATION

i only wrote
these words
to make the man
who told you
he was a poet
less of a liar.

WINNIE LEE

she was sweet iced cream, a shadow dream
for the men she tried to please
a weathervane framed in moonlight
a silhouette on the trees

she left home for a taste of silk and lace
not sheltered from those things
that steal your heart so silently
like a raven's flapping wing

she rose in the south, set in the west
like sun that forgot how to shine
her path went stray, she lost her way
like songs that lose their rhyme

winnie lee   winnie be   winnie hear this plea
winnie see   winnie we can never be free
winnie woe   winnie when will it come again
winnie where   winnie why   winnie please don't cry

now thoughts erase when lost to the wind
set adrift by every breeze
but return to haunt a midnight jaunt
and bend her heart till it bleeds

some day she'll lay in the morning dew
start again seeding the tree
that grows to a woman that knows her pride
whose hand bears the brand: winnie lee

some day she'll say all lies are like weeds
so feed them flowers and tea
and go with a woman that glows with pride
whose hand bares the brand: winnie lee.

AT THE NUNNERY

womb of granite
graveyard poem

withdrawn from laughter
carnal foam

heart throbs
desire moans

groans of fire
blood and bone

sighs from heaven
thighs of chrome

cries and whispers
froze in stone.

HOW THE DEVIL ESCORTED
LENNIE CHIVERS TO PARADISE

fixing a stare wooden and square
he spoke so brave and free
we'll go to my place, dress in lace
and see what there is to see

we'll wash in wine and drink champagne
watch the sun and sea
we'll read a rhyme from ancient time
and touch the imagery

she thought it kinky and with a wink
she smiled so sexy and said
i may be crazy and sometimes lazy
but i'll take my chance in bed

so they sang a stanza from mario lanza
while scorpio rose from the dead
and after dinner she knew he'd win her
with magic wine and bread

that night the lovers while under cover
discovered where loving had led
their bodies reclined and every touch rhymed
so silver cloud linings were shed

and when their pleasure surrendered treasure
to a morning of amber and gold
they both remembered the verse from december
and the passion a song could unfold.

ADRIFT NEAR CANNERY ROW

whispers of rain
flutter on soft gray wings
across the redwood bay
where waves hide in hollow caves
waiting for the song of whales

and when it's time
this dance of silver feathers
will hunt for hungry clouds
lost as a stitch in time
and fly, fly
to chimneys of the sky.

LOVE DRUNK

love drunk
for the 44th time
this week alone

every time is like the 1st

love drunk
in my blood is like whiskey
in a navajo

every time is like the 1st

love drunk
you can bet i won't take the cure
raleigh hills is out

every time is like the 1st

love drunk
i'll eat dinosaurs by day
slay dragons in the night
and die in a twisted knot

but i'll stay love drunk
'cause every time is like the 1st
yeah, every time is like the 1st.

BLOOD RITE

come let our words be razors
cutting through skin and paper
like typewriter keys that punch holes
where the periods should have been
letting in light or letting out blood
for the readers or the writers

then we will fuse this legion of razors
and forge great pens of blue steel
carefully honed
well tempered
hand hammered
scratching history from skin
carving legends from bone

and i will be that bone
this legend of a working class hero
and you can be the skin
a history book well shaped by revolution
a study in economics
where the size of reward
equals the sum of sacrifice

and we might grow fat & rich
by shaving thin strips of our epidermis
and carefully trading each morsel for a word
and exchanging minor limbs for major songs
and selling entire vital organs
[broken hearts excluded]
for a real gem of a novel

[which might be a bag of tricks]
bartering our lives
for a poem no one reads.

THE EDUCATION OF THE MASTER RACE

we are educated
the master race

architects
building gas chambers

chemists
poisoning women

surgeons
carving up men

generals
murdering children

statesmen
incinerating a nation

we are educated
the master race.

BLACK LIGHT

from the black light
i heard an old voice
liquid smooth from blood in the throat
spitting songs tattood by broken bone
and corrugated by standing up and falling down

from the black light
i heard an old voice
that sadly sang of things that died
reincarnation
the second time around
creases under enamel eyes
and no longer perfect breasts

and then
from the black light
i heard a new voice
that sang with the music
i had danced to from orpheus
and scars and old echoes faded
into a light of the whitest white

from the white light
i heard a new voice
from the white light
i heard you sing.

HOODOO VOODOO

"Corruptio optimi pessima."[1]

i'll fabricate a golem
from gehenna will come this drone
a means to the genius of power
a willing supernatural clone

i'll enclose myself in a circle
chant spells of the bal shem tov
place butterflies on my shoulder
raise my palms to the sky above

i'll lace my neck in hexagrams
sing verses from cabala
dance naked in the midnight moon
and listen for the raven's caw

i'll blend mandrake, mortar, straw
stir mud and blood and stone
study abulafia
carve charms of chinese bone

i'll hoodoo demon voodoo
mix a mumbo jumbo plan
my golem slave will bring me all
from circe's ancient land

and when accused of crime or sin
apostasy or whim
i'll blame the golem crying, god believe
it was not me, it was him.

[1] The corruption of the best is the worst of all.

THE SMOKE OF
DISTANT DREAMS

the dreams of mayday macintosh
exploded like shooting stars
into the swamp of a black georgia night
and she felt her past become diffused
as if viewed through white surgical gauze
differentiation
between autobiography and dream propaganda
was only a razor cut
and really real moments as these
were then but an uncertainty.

ALL DAY PARKING

Just down from 3rd on Broadway, Carlos ran the self-park. He wore a large, gold crucifix and faded jeans a size too tight. He had nice eyes and was very handsome so the Catholic mothers would cross themselves whenever he passed their daughters. But Carlos was respectable. He drove a late model BMW while his best friend obsessed over a primer gray Chevy with diamond tuck interior and tinted windows. I once thought Carlos was *cholo* like the other *homeboys* who wore baggy chinos to make you wonder if they had a weapon hidden in their pockets, to make you wonder if they were tough, *muy peligroso*. But that was all very long ago.

When Carlos got excited he would stammer as he talked. Then he would get embarrassed and go quiet. He had done *hard time* but would never talk of it. I heard it from Ramona, one of his two sisters, both covergirl pretty. A brother had been killed in a gang war, quarreling over whose turf was whose. Death in exchange for fifty yards of ground and some extra cockroaches in the cornmeal. And when Ramona was raped, Carlos and his one remaining brother cruised by on that sweltering Saturday night and shotgunned the son-of-a-bitch right off the sidewalk. Right in front of his home, while he was drinking a can of beer. Right in front of his mother.

But Carlos was a model prisoner and became a trustee. And after sixty months in Soledad, he pulled parole. The self-park was his reprieve. He loved that place. He could be on the street and watch life sweat and bleed. And be part of it. He shaved his moustache. He did not need to prove his freedom. He did not run from *La Migre*. Thirty years before, when his mother was a *bracero*, she waded across the Rio Grande and went into labor in the red, Texas mud. Carlos was born an American. He was legal.

And when Ramona was a baby, her tiny legs were brittle with polio. Doctors prescribed injections and braces, and waited for her to grow out of it. But her mother did not wait. Mrs. Ramirez prayed every day to The Virgin and on Easter

90

crawled to the church on hand and knee, leaving a trail of skin and blood. In four months her wounds healed and baby Ramona started walking. Mrs. Ramirez thanked the blessed Virgin for saving her daughter, and the doctors stopped the injections.

Ramona also was very devout. She would cross herself before I sucked her breasts, murmur Hail Marys while we fucked, buck her hips wildly, scream profanities, and come like an early train. Then she would turn away for a moment, cry quietly and cross herself some more. I loved her. She was fifteen, and maybe for her Indian blood, her pussy always smelled good. When Carlos found us together, he called me a bastard and vowed to kill me. Then his warm eyes confessed his love and he laughed. He was like the brother I would have favored.

And because it was winter, Carlos let a friend sleep in the parking shed. But the friend was illegal and was sent back to Mexico. And Carlos was sent before the parole board. He had broken the rules.

Then things happened much too fast. Carlos chose Viet Nam instead of prison and made me swear not to let his self-park go under. Ramona wrote to him daily, fucked me sore and went to confession. In July a letter came from the government: Carlos had been killed in a mined rice paddy. He was handsome, and he was smart, but he was never lucky Their mama aged ten years in a day and wore black the remainder of her life. Carlos had been the favorite. Ramona took her vows and joined the convent at Holy Cross. I see her now, once every third Sunday. She wears a grey habit and rarely speaks. Me, I drink beer and talk with the street people on Broadway. The flies dance near the photo of Carlos that I keep over the timeclock in the self-park shed. I could never bear to sell it.

A SPASM OF BLACK

embracing
an hourglass of inky night
his tall heart quivered with ruin
as sable lips kissed
his palm of gold
and in a glimpse of heaven
the black widow became
mother, sister and lover
as ebony feet smaller than rain
tickled his finger
and the clutch of cold diamond belly
excited him
and his nostrils flared
and his blood pumped thickly
and in a spasm of black
her poison exploded in his ruby veins
and in that trance of death, he froze
and so, she owned his soul.

THE LAST WAVE

I

the wave came high and alone
and far from another sea
where the language of men
was not remembered

and it came with white fingers
to sweep the land
clean, west to los angeles
kansas, new york

and we saw the water curl
with frothy peaks now ten feet high
and so, with glass boards nailed
to our backs like crosses at calvary
we slowly, slowly
dragged across the sand
to the cool atonement of sea

and cutting through walls
and canyons of tall kelp
the waters grew
fatter, fatter
bulging like a pregnant god
about to give birth

and so we came, an eastern swell
ten, twenty, thirty feet
foaming into midday
and the island of granite
with hills soon flat
and barely rolling

and the voice of water was everywhere
and our arms grew black with sunlight

II

and at sixty feet
i piloted the last wave in
glued to my board like a rocket seat
and yet, no wind passed my ears
as i shot through the water
like a feather in a vacuum
toward the beach
on the crest of the great wave

and i prayed and prayed
for the beach to be forgiving
as wet sand is to a clam's bubble
and i prayed not to come out
of the chute head down
with a billion pounds
of water on my back

sand would not forgive me then
it would rise up and smash me
the way mountain smashes airplane
and my face would explode

and with those prayers
came quick deliverance
and i sledded over dunes of sand
skimming like a flat grunion
and the wave behind me grew
higher, higher

Also by Scott Sonders:

RAZOR CANDY
CALIFORNIA DREAMGIRLS

Walking in Stone

John Spaulding
Walking in Stone

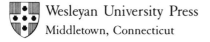 Wesleyan University Press
Middletown, Connecticut

Twelve of these sections previously appeared in a chapbook by the author entitled *The Roses of Starvation* (Riverstone Press, 1987). Others appeared in *The Ark*, *Blue Buildings*, *Prickly Pear* (Tucson), and *The Written ARTS*.

Substantial portions of this work were completed at the Virginia Center for the Creative Arts and the Millay Colony for the Arts, and the author gratefully acknowledges the opportunities afforded by these colonies.

All inquiries and permissions requests should be addressed to the Publisher, Wesleyan University Press, 110 Mt. Vernon Street, Middletown, Connecticut 06457

LIBRARY OF CONGRESS CATALOGING-IN-PUBLICATION DATA

Spaulding, John.
   Walking in stone / John Spaulding.
     p. cm.
   Bibliography: p.
   ISBN 0-8195-2174-4   ISBN 0-8195-1176-5 (pbk.)
   I. Title.
PS3569.P379W35   1989
811'.54—dc19   88-31768
               CIP

Manufactured in the United States of America

First Edition

Wesleyan New Poets

To Anne and Cylor

Contents

I

The Impingement

The air breathes upon us here most sweetly

The Tempest, II, i

I

I suppose it is happening that way
Someplace floating islands come
small islands with tall trees
slowly through the black sea
bringing their clouds their birds
and someone wants to go to them
wants to walk on their soft earth
pick their ground berries
hunt their squirrels
Someone wants to drift with them a while
rest on their rocks
Someone wants to float with them
Someone wants to float with them
to that place
I suppose it is happening that way

2

Knuckle of God. Dominion of flint
and fat and lusty soils. Great
pink-barked trees. Huge bones
and whale ribs on the beach. Bushels
of sassafras for French pox. Our
shining light on this island
laden with grapes.

Burnt forests. Acres of shores shell-heaped.
Battlefields of wild people. Pigeon-darkened skies.
Rivers stuffed with fat shad, eel, salmon.
Wolves heads for the meeting house door.
The air—cold, raw, searching.

3

Who is holding onto the bark from the inside of trees
the dark berries from inside the bush
Why do you ask for the rotten-corn place and
the clam-cooking place and as well
the property of raccoons
The black people why did you bring them they
walk around like pieces of night
Why did you come here did you run out of firewood
in your place of living
Are you feeling sorry for those pigs that you made
running around on that island

4

We are the knife people, iron men, coat people
    and he-lands-sailing.
Souse eaters, house makers, husbands
    of kine and goat and swine, farm builders
    and keepers of kettle and scummer, word
    scratchers, corn stealers and bad sleepers.

As if towns could build themselves.
As if stumps jumped from the ground or
    flesh of beasts fell into trenchers.
As if paradise prevailed on earth.
To come to rich moulds and lush plantings,
    long-necked trees and tongues of land,

to redd the wild for the unborn.
    To reck not the peril.
Suffering snakes that may fly, wolves
    that may ravish. Kingdom
    of sachem and sagamore.
Kingdom of corn and thorny promise.

To satisfy our appetite of spirit,
    our thirst of property.
To seek not the opera of war but
    belittled by the possibilities
to stand silenced by the task before us —

these be my sudden and undigested thoughts.

5

Who forgets things and has to go back
who is covered by a fur of dark clouds a skin of fear
who settles down on old mats of leaves
and dreams of his youth
who spends a long time sleeping
who separates time between here and there
who makes noises with his teeth
and drops things from the tops of trees
who wants to live in the sky

Who holds things in his mouth
and goes home to swallow

6

And then they compelled him to sing which he did.
A very sad song. Afterward they administered firebrands
to his skin, tore off fingernails, put fire
to his private parts as well as to his bleeding fingerends.
Flogged his head and poured on pitch then pierced
his wrists to tear out sinew.
Sounds came from his mouth.

When I could not stomach this
I shot the wild man. But it did not end.
For they opened his belly and tossed
entrails to the different directions yet
keeping the headskin. Finally cut up the heart
to force it into the mouth of his brother.
After seeing these things I bathed in spirits of wine,

drank chalybeate with castor and tent wine. And
balsam of fennel for my violent fevers.
But my eyes remained with the sight and
would not wash away with the spectacles of the sea
nor the vast rivers of the North. I dreamed
long dreams of the man for many years
and I did not marry.

7

Over there those people are walking in stone
up to their knees
Over there those people are changing
Over there those people are changing into
snail and eel they are fighting in that lake
they have fought so hard on account of that
they have stirred up the lake all furious
so now it is all muddy and confused so
they will probably call it Confused Lake now
Over there those people are pointing their fingers
and saying 'you will see something before long'
making everyone small and running away
and that is how it is over there

8

At six I knew the names of the kingdoms,
the lineage of Ruth,
everlastings that frosted the grange.
Now I hear the flute of the natives come night—
wauls, chucks, drones and scrapes.
Dream of flour and windows and friends.
The worm of sleep eating my mind.
We have all changed shape here—
Dear God you would not know us.

9

Ways of living on the warming earth
    He comes within sight he becomes visible he is born
    Someone enters the lodge and someone says 'there is room'
    He discovers his footprint
    His eating is fat he is satisfied with what is given to him
    He blows with the mouth he restores life to himself
    He is in a place he is there

Ways of living somewhere else
    He occupies too much room
    He sinks down into the trough of the sea
    He is not satisfied with what is given to him
    He makes an end of eating
    He is raised up by the wind
    He is transparent he can be seen through

10

Oysters twelve inches long, 200 kinds
of fish and lobsters upwards of 25 pounds:
Write of this: 'fish abound and can be killed
by striking with sticks, by horses hooves
as they ford streams' but drink now our famine
broth of snow, deerskin and smoke, and
sometime remember the roses of starvation,
fulgent blossoms of pellagra that
open on the skin of our dead.

II

The Turning

When is death not within ourselves?

Heraclitus

I

In the spring time the stars began looking for him
By summer time they had found him
By autumn time they had wounded him
    so that the orange and red of his blood began
    to leak from the sky onto the leaves of the trees
By winter time they had slain him
    so that his white fat began to melt and drip
    falling as snow all over the land

And then he would begin to rise again
    first as sap in the trees
    stretching higher and higher
until his back ached but
    knowing he would not stop until
    his black fur was hidden
    deep among the unborn
behind the dark wall of the night sky

2

The real farmers are all dead.
Their earthen fingers and toes
work the ground around them.
They eat the soil as the soil eats them
working both day and night
plowing the turgid earth
while cries of 'Slothfulness! Slothfulness!'
wrack the air.

3

That man makes the moose hiding under bushes
That man makes a canoe out of rock
That man freezes his enemies
He is stamping his feet into ice and hard earth
He makes himself floating in the air
He makes himself hiding in the sleep of deep water

He wanders around
He drinks tobacco
He jumps up to the growing point of trees
He is not afraid of the others
He is careful about things

4

Pendulum of jerked flesh. Rocking stone.
Skinbag of gore. Staring at earth. Hands and feet
gnawed. Pismires struggling through
white hairs and cassock. An old man hanged himself
and was dead. This the sight: Face empurpled,
bowels evacuated.

Windlestraw.
Windlestraw.

5

Now when the world became dark all over
everything started to turn red
everywhere there was roaring
the words drowned and all
the black bears came running toward the sea
all the deer went toward the sea
and also cougars wolves foxes and catamounts
the hair on all of them was partly burnt
also their legs and tails
We found holes in the ground and crawled in
as wave after wave swept our backs
for eight days it was dark all over
and we were alone and broken like weeds
at the bottom of the sea

6

Gatherings of dyestuff. Not scarlet, famous all over
  the medieval world. From Europe ships with indigo
  crossing the raven-colored sea.

Not gallnuts—'woody swellings caused by attacks
  of gallflies on old oak.' Neither saffron nor weld
  for yellow nor madder for red. Through the years

the most enduring. But for beige use lungwort.
  Picked off the ground in any season after a storm.
  Finally black. Extract of night pulled from poison ivy

that our rasping grief might torment the snow.

7

The wind has come that you can see and smell
it is the boiling month and all
over the North the grandfathers
are called the children are called the
hunters and trappers are called
the beaver and moose and Abenaki and
Kennebec are called while ravens float
through the perfumed air near their pines
the otter sleeps beside his soft parents and death
drifts through the night and day like snow again
and again the voice comes over
our heads saying the People are dying in great
numbers over there the People are dying
over there and some leave infected
areas in canoes eating roots and ducklings
and some drag their burning bodies to
the shore and everywhere the smell of tobacco
we are all much alarmed someone has said
that this may be the end of us all but someone
has seen our descendants coming toward us

8

An old man was found sitting in his grave
boiling stones a little before candlelight.
After meeting Mrs. Whitney was seen crying in the orchard.
Much lightning at night for many days.

Contemplate the growing extravagance of velvet and scarlet
among the people of low rank.
Contemplate the complaints against you
the new singing and the wearing of your wig.

Notice the earth begin to move sometime before dawn
reported extremely heavy to the north.
Then the rain.
Then the worms crawling over the crops.

9

Something has entered my thinking and my talking

Even when we are not near the mountains
    the bear people come hungry and thirsty
    they frisk about in a certain way
    they rub up against trees

Who is speaking to me now

I have pain in some part of my body
I am bitten by flies or lice

Someone is talking about religious matters
He is not one of the principal people

I have gone too deep into the mountains
I awaken with violence

10

Eelwives and pickerel. Salmon. I know the leafmold
    and rime near my setting place. Amoskeag Falls.
    Where I go to for days and fish at night.

I buy a musquash skin. 5 shad for a quart of rum and 4 eels
    for a pint that I paid to drink in the night. For one
    half a ten lb salmon we get a glass bottle full of rum.

Remember cinnamon and heckled flax. Ink powder and nails.
    I hunt bees in the afternoon.

At James Littles barn raising Vyler Anderson got killed he
    never breathed the blood ran so fast at his ears and
        mouth.
    Saw a blazing star. I see it about an hour below the
    7 stars. Whitish the star small. This forenoon I lay by.

plesant foggy morning. Clouded and thundered and had a
    smart
        shower about noon and we came home and I killed 3
        pidgeons.

III

The Stand

*The world . . . ever was, and is, and shall be,
ever-living Fire, in measures being kindled
and in measures going out.*

Heraclitus

I

On the same day
I saw a meal of parched corn a kettle of groundnuts boiling
I saw the box where they would keep the sickness
the bag of peace made from bitter hemp
I saw the accretions of their lives
    the remains of the design of amity as well as
    the removal of persons from their proper stations
    the people disgraced with begging

And the man said 'you can see the pain'
and the clouds came and went away again
and the people believed in nothing
    were without manners when they ate their corn
    and when they relieved themselves of their water
    in front of the others
and the children made no noise and did not play
    as though childhood itself were damaged in some way
    as though they had no hope in hope itself
and the ashes of something were all around
    their homes their campground their places of fire
    and even their feet and legs when they walked
like grey leaves dried and blowing all around

And the man said 'they die like rotten sheep over here—
    they die like rotten sheep'—
    the experience of something they had been through

2

From running away
from his lawful master
again and again then returning
to live with them,
his parents were duly warned by the court
to keep John Walker, age five,
bound to his lawful master
or be set in pillory.
From frequent and unreasonable beatings
with the back covered in stripes,
the skin blackish and blue
and broken in various places,—
From deprivations of food and clothings
and demands for heavy work
beyond his years from which
he did constantly wet his bedding and nightclothes
and frozen were these things
about his body when found—
John Walker, age thirteen, servant,
is now returned to his Rightful Master.

3

Overlooking the failed battleground
beseeching the small stones to say nothing
the land and the grass to be silent
Only the wind that pockets the smell of 600
burnt Pequots—flaunts it—
none covered nor buried—here a broken tooth
half burnt arm

Seven of us sup on a fish they call pout
and did not eat it up
Our thin and bitter fingers rinsing themselves
in the swamp—saying nothing

The wind that runs over our roasted brothers our village
snakes crawling out of the roughage
across our toes—women finding
a few pots blackened but still good

Each boy finding his own grandfather
his own grandmother

Tonight a black frost
The winter will eat us quickly
saying nothing

4

Wife being oppressed with every illness: procidentia
   uteri, mouth obstructed, breast broken, shivering
   and trembling and vomiting and flux. Rising
   from her bed she is sewn together by pain.

Babe ceased to breathe about bedtime. Young neighbor
   dug the grave. Snow very deep. First death
   in my family. May God enable me to see his sovereign
      mind.
   That weeping may not hinder sowing.

5

Cut ankle while chopping wood. Bled very much.
Cold time and the time of great hunger.
Tried puff ball to staunch the bleeding.
Filled the sore with sugar. No success.
Tried scraps of tanned leather.
Then scorched cotton. Still fresh puddles appeared.

The smell of raw meat or ghosts.
Finally someone came. A giant with a heart of ice.
Turning people into something.
Eating people. Even his own family.
When the ground began to show itself again
the whole camp was white with bone.

6

By the decrease in your strength,
the shrinkage of sinews,
by the spotting of your flesh with bloody spots,
by the stink of your breath, the rotting
away of the gums at the roots of teeth,
by the final blow of death
will you know the pestilence come among you,
then should you cause some one to be ripped open
and mark the heart rotten with red water
about it the lungs black and mortified rotten blood
bursting out the heart and
spleen somewhat rough and perished,
then should you boil up some spruce needles and speak
to some one with concern for your race, the
evening of its life saying
this great amen at last to
the long and thoughtless prayer
that is your living.

7

When they come in from the hunt
they drink and fight—
spending their skins
neglect their farming—they sleep
and remain like that for days

And when the dogs come
in the night where people lie uncovered
the dogs that eat up dead things
and the people are full of strong water
their fire catches their houses
sticks to everything
won't let go
the new flies come that like that smell
to crawl over their bodies
and their children cry their houses burn
in time of sun rising
the rope of something is around their necks

8

The leaves were dripping in the darkness
and wolves were gathering.
The path to the river was like grease from the rain
and lightning had left a sulfurous vapor in the air.
There was little to eat except for cakes
crumbling in our pockets and a buck
left on a tree by those who had gone on ahead.
All dogs had been strangled before we left to silence them.
'Buildings burned and cattle and hogs killed'—
'Buildings burned and cattle and hogs killed'—
These words excited continual fears.

9

By facing the earth and tasting
the delicacy of the sweet soils
survived being knocked on the head
and scalpt easily the hair
slid off as though cut by someone but
thought the skull had opened

the afterbrain ready to pour out.
Soon congealed the wound a terrible
tightness there couldn't bear
touching it with hands or fingers and
feet so very sore from walking each night
wrung blood from the stockings when

peeling them off. Then the skin come off
from the ankle whole like a shoe and
left the toes naked without nails
the ends turning black. I was obliged
to cut the first joint off with a knife.
Thought I should die but now

someone is walking across the world
in stinking clothes
snowflakes falling carefully around his head.

IO

Severed heads and hands planted
on poles in our path—
how should we react to this?
Our young messenger's
head hurled as a foot ball before our eyes—
how should we react to this?
We cannot encompass these things
into our daily round
into our corn grinding our sleep or salt making
into our reflection of what life is
or how to live our lives.
We say it is from another course of living
and we talk about this to God.
He has told someone this is indeed Satan's land
that he has lived here for centuries.
Undiscovered.
These wild men are Satan's children.
Why they are benumbed and dirty and without garment.
Why they have no government no body of law.
Why their words are long and opaque.
Why they die in great numbers after our brief visits.
Because they cannot survive our goodness.

IV

The Aftersong

. . . when I waked
I cried to dream again

The Tempest, III, ii

I

3 men whipt 80 lashes a piece and
a woman 52 lashes on bare rump
then drummed out of camp.

Had a great rarity for dinner
and that a steamed pudding.
Something else howls.

Is it the sky boiling with fat pidgeons
or God's minions flooding the heavens
to sing this bloody piece of work?

When my wind is spent my body breached
then will I lie down to die
under great angry trees.

2

The old people when they get sick
they want to know where we will put them
if they will be left for the enemy to see
or if they will be covered up and facing the right way

They are always with us always watching us the enemy
in our sleep and creeping up after us the enemy
at night we hear frogs and crickets listening to them
they poke around they spy on us
they try to find out what we eat every day
what we put in our stew
they try to discover where we have been
so that now we do not go back we do not look back
there is nothing behind us but enemy
walking so close it is like our own past
our own story hungry to swallow us

Nothing behind us but enemy
and those things
those things we toss in its mouth

3

Once in moonlight when I had not slept for three nights,
when there was no food and a long rain had stopped,
and some had slept outside in the rain you could see
the streaks it had left on their skin,
once in the eighth week of my captivity,
alone in the moonlight outside on the ledge,
I looked up and felt the stars move
strangely back and forth, a slow rocking,
as though the Lord were rocking us somehow back and forth,
and I was not afraid but tears came anyway
as I remembered my children so far away,
the way children can call you back
in through your thoughts and keep you awake
like hearing the stars ring all night long.
And when you watch animals die,
when deer die you notice it,
how they don't cry out—
I could see it in my mind's eye—
they don't cry out but lie there, eyes open,
and then they are dead outside of themselves
they are dead but inside themselves
they have joined the earth where they have always been
rocking and rocking.—And so
I was able to sleep a few hours before our next remove,
miles and miles beyond the Great River,
though I had lost track of our place in the world.

4

That big ship is gone now the one that was here
It moves slowly away slowly moving somewhere
    full of people
His woman and his child the ones that were taken
      when picking berries over there those people
      over there where there are birds and berries
They are being taken somewhere
Somebody is buying them far away for something

And his head is still up there
They cut off his head and they cut off his hands
    and they are still up there
They broke up the rest of him like that
      and they put pieces of him on trees and poles
      and they left them there and they are still up there

And those birds come around here and we watch them
      following that ship for a long time
      until it is far away that ship way over there
Those birds are looking for more of those berries they said
They taste so they said they have that flavor they said

5

As dark as it has been with us
it becomes darker still.
A caul over our sluggish minds.
Our tabetic flesh
tempted by the earth's soft fleece
and pressure of sleep.
New fruit on the branches of death,
the hearts of women and children—
wild red berries,
dark blue plums.

6

The people call out from the noise of the earth

They paint their faces black and cut their hair
They plant small trees around
They cry out and cut their arms

The people call out from the noise of the earth
And he is singing somewhere the Owner and he sings
Quietly he sings 'do not be afraid' in his song he tells us that
Sometimes at night the people hear that the singing

It goes so
It goes so singing

7

At first we thought we were of angels—
whenever we asked for deliverance we accompanied ourselves
prancing like piglets gorging on fat.
In the coverture of this time where no one sees
in the grume of our faith
in the distress of beasts
tempered by pinching want
we become weapons of our immane desire
biding the yellow night.
We are less than our hymns or these
whispers of walnut ink tell of us.

8

Nobody lives there now
Nobody lives there now where they were living
Maybe their houses burned down there now a while ago
Anyway those places grew up with trees and bushes and
    broomstraw
and the pathways disappeared a while ago
and those people are all gone now
the flint people the people at white pine place
the dawn land people and the ones who broke up
and the people at great hill those people
are all gone now a long time they have been gone
They have been quiet a long time
They don't have to build morning fires there anymore
and anyway they don't need to go hunting anymore
or catch beaver or eel or build lodges
and they don't have to run after moose anymore
and anyway they don't have to move before the snow comes
Nobody goes over there now

9

A stumpful of water. A gramarye of silence
in the dusky drift of animalism.
As if the light is put out and there is
sitting in the darkness as if a great tree
had fallen and its weight had put out the fire.
Life abides by snowlight.
A spoonful of broth. A lump of bearmeat.
Intimations of glazy death
in the slow fall of history's water:
the endless music of memory.

10

In those days we wandered about
No cows—no sheep—full of fish
and questions we began to look around
We heard of something
far away like smoke rising

An old man had seen a small green worm
drop down from a birch branch
The thin rope he had made himself
When he touched earth
he climbed back again

That drum we carried with us—swollen
by rain and sorrow it was so near
we had forgotten to look there

Notes

NOTES

In the manner of what might be called "documentary poetry," this work both pulls from and chronicles the events of seventeenth-century New England—particularly the blending of native peoples and European colonists. Although a few sources lie outside either the century or the topography, they fall enough within the ethos of the period to warrant their use. Yet, as with any reconstruction, the whole remains a somewhat mythical piece of real estate. The following provided specific source material:

1. 1. When they first saw sailing ships, some native people in New England thought they were floating islands. See Wood, W. *New Englands Prospect*. Amsterdam: DaCapo Press, 1968. (First published in 1634.)

1. 2. Suggested by Brereton, J. *A briefe and True Relation . . . of the North part of Virginia, with an intro. note by Luther S. Livingston*. New York: Dodd, Mead & Co., 1903. (First published in 1602.)

1. 3. The terms "rotten-corn place" and "clam-cooking place," as well as the last four lines were suggested by pages in Cronon, W. *Changes in the Land: Indians, Colonists, and the Ecology of New England*. New York: Hill & Wang, 1983.

1. 4. "Knife people," "iron men," "coat people," and "he-lands-sailing" were all terms used by native people to describe the English. The last line was taken from Bridenbaugh, C. (Ed.). *The Pynchon Papers, Vol. 1: Letters of John Pynchon, 1654–1700*. Boston: The Colonial Society of Massachusetts, 1982.

1. 6. Based upon one of the experiences of Champlain. See Bourne, E. G. (Ed.). *The Voyages and Explorations of Samuel de Champlain, 1604–1616. Narrated by Himself*. Trans. by A. N. Bourne. Vol. 1. New York: Allerton Book Co., 1922.

1. 7. Derived from material in Speck, F. G. *Penobscot Shamanism*.

Memoirs of the American Anthropological Ass'n. Vol. 6, no. 4 (Oct.–Dec. 1919).

I. 10. The term "roses of starvation" to describe the skin eruptions of pellagra has been attributed to a seventeenth-century French physician. This information and the "broth of snow, deerskin and smoke," as well as inspiration for this poem came from Josephy, A. M., Jr. (Ed.). *The American Heritage Book of Indians.* New York: American Heritage Publishing Co., 1961.

II. 1. Utilizes Mahican lore. See Jones, E. *Stockbridge, Past and Present; or Records of an Old Mission Station.* Springfield, MA: Samuel Bowles, 1854.

II. 5. Suggested by a passage in Fractenberg, L. J. *Alsea Texts and Myths.* Smithsonian Institution, Bureau of American Ethnology, Bulletin 67, Washington, D.C., 1920.

II. 6. The quotation "woody swellings . . ." and other material related to dyeing were obtained from Schetky, E. McD. (Ed.). *Dye Plants and Dyeing: A Handbook.* Baltimore: Brooklyn Botanic Garden, 1964.

II. 7. Based upon a passage in Densmore, F. *Chippewa Customs.* Reprint ed. St. Paul: Minnesota Historical Society Press, 1979. (First published in 1929.)

II. 8. The third line and the second stanza are based upon certain entries in Walett, F. G. (Ed.). *The Diary of Ebenezer Parkman, First Part, 1719–1755.* Worcester, MA: American Antiquarian Society, 1974.

II. 10. Utilizes material from various odd entries in Patten, M. *The Diary of Matthew Patten of Bedford, N. H.* Concord, NH: Town of Bedford, 1903.

III. 1. The quotation "they die like rotten sheep" is a description used by William Bradford in a somewhat different context. Davis, W. T. (Ed.). *Bradford's History of Plymouth Plantation, 1606–1646.* New York: Barnes and Noble, 1946.

III. 2. Drawn from the story of John Walker as described in Demos, J. *A Little Commonwealth: Family Life in Plymouth Colony.* London:

Oxford University Press, 1970. Demos reports that Walker's master was eventually convicted of manslaughter and was sentenced to have his goods confiscated and his hand burned (p. 114).

III. 3. In 1637 some 500 to 700 Pequots were burned alive by the English.

III. 4. Profits from assorted entries in Walett, F. G. (Ed.). *The Diary of Ebenezer Parkman, First Part, 1719–1755.* Worcester, MA: American Antiquarian Society, 1974.

III. 5. The first stanza is based upon an entry in Walett, F. G. (Ed.) *The Diary of Ebenezer Parkman, First Part, 1719–1755.* Worcester, MA: American Antiquarian Society, 1974. The second stanza employs the Windigo legend of the northern Algonquian-speaking peoples.

III. 6. A general description of scurvy as adapted from a passage in Wright, L. B., and Fowler, E. W. (Eds.). *West and by North: North America Seen Through the Eyes of Its Seafaring Discoverers.* New York: Delacorte Press, 1971.

III. 8. Drawn from an incident described in *Green Mountain Whittlins: Bicentennial Edition.* Essex Junction, VT: Green Mountain Folklore Society, 1975.

III. 9. The sentence in the third stanza which begins "Then the skin come off . . ." is almost a direct quotation of a sentence in Gyles, J. *Memoirs of Odd Adventures, Strange Deliverances, Etc.* Boston, 1736, as reprinted in Vaughn, A. T., and Clark, E. W. (Eds.). *Puritans Among the Indians.* Cambridge: Harvard University Press, 1981.

III. 10. That the native people were considered children of Satan by many of the colonists is well documented. See, for example, Segal, C. M., and Stineback, D. C. *Puritans, Indians and Manifest Destiny.* New York: G. P. Putnam's Sons, 1977.

IV. 3. Suggested by the captivity of Mary Rowlandson as it is reprinted in Lincoln, C. H. (Ed.). *Narratives of the Indian Wars, 1675–1699.* New York: Charles Scribner's Sons, 1913.

IV. 4. Before King Philip's (Metacomet's) War ended, his wife and son were captured in a berry patch. They were later sold into slavery across the sea.

IV. 9. *Cf.* "The sachem is looked upon as a great tree under whose shade the whole nation is sit"—the words of Captain Hendrick Aupaumut as quoted in Jones, E. *Stockbridge, Past and Present; or Records of an Old Mission Station.* Springfield, MA: Samuel Bowles, 1854.

ABOUT THE AUTHOR

John Spaulding's book is, in a sense, a mythic story of his own roots. His family had emigrated to New England in 1750; one of his ancestors was a Native American. He was born in Hanover, New Hampshire; since 1982 he has been a clinical psychologist with Native North American peoples in Ontario, Oklahoma, and Arizona, where he served at the Phoenix Indian Medical Center. Now in the state of Washington, he is chief of mental health and social services for the Puget Sound Service Unit of the Indian Health Service. He has also worked as an editor, at the University of Arizona Press, and taught high-school English, in Pomona, California.

Spaulding received two M.A.'s, in English and in psychology, and a Ph.D., in psychology, from the University of Arizona, Tucson. He has received two awards from the Academy of American Poets, a fellowship from the Millay Colony for the Arts, in 1987, and an achievement award from the U.S. Public Health Service, also in 1987. This is his first book. His home is in Maple Valley, Washington.

ABOUT THE BOOK

Walking in Stone was composed on the Mergenthaler 202 in Granjon, a typeface designed for Linotype by George W. Jones, an English printer. It is neither a copy of a classic face nor an original creation, but something between the two, with its basic design stemming from classic Garamond sources.

The book was composed by Marathon Typography Service, Inc. in Durham, North Carolina, and designed and produced by Kachergis Book Design, Pittsboro, North Carolina.